Drive & Learn
SPANISH
NEW EDITION

by Howard Beckerman

FALL RIVER PRESS

This edition published by Fall River Press, by arrangement with APA Publications GmbH & Co. Verlag Products

Drive & Learn is an exclusive Fall River Press edition based on APA's *Rush Hour* series.

Fall River Press
122 Fifth Avenue
New York, NY 10011

Senior Acquisitions Editor: *Sheryl Olinsky Borg*
Editor: *Juergen Lorenz*
Orchestrations: *Tru Doty*
Audio Production: *Heartworks International, Inc., Stony Brook, NY*
Senior French Language Consultant: *Thierry Royo*
Voice Talent: *Guylaine Laperrière, Michel Chevalier, Jim Brannigan, Sher Alexi Komisar, Jack Walker, Freddy Penha, Teresa Labarga, Cathy Bolz, Amy Raupp, Paul Ehlers, Howard Beckerman, Bri Beckerman, Josh Beckerman, and Linda Beckerman*
Interior Design and Layout: *Wee Design Group*

ISBN 0-7607-8983-5

Printed in U.S.A.

Table of Contents

Introduction

Drive & Learn Spanish is a musical language program that uses the power of catchy melodies and dynamic rhythms to introduce you to basic Spanish expressions and vocabulary for daily life. As you will quickly discover, ***Drive & Learn Spanish*** is not a grammar course. There are no rules to memorize here! The method is simple and direct: Listen, repeat, and if you wish, sing along! The musical styles are diverse and the language-learning process is quick and enjoyable.

The ***Drive & Learn Spanish*** audio "shows" in this program are designed to be listened to again and again for your language-learning pleasure and progress. You will soon find yourself speaking Spanish without effort, as you follow our lead character Jon through all the events of his day. And as Jon learns Spanish, so will you, with the assistance of a very unusual Spanish teacher—and original music that will attune you to the language so that it sticks with you.

The bilingual ***Drive & Learn*** approach will ease you into the language as you hear words and expressions first in English and then in Spanish. And although reading is not required for the ***Drive & Learn*** experience, for additional support, the entire script and song lyrics are included in this Listener's Guide, along with ***Drive & Learn*** vocabulary and phrase sections and a mini-grammar for quick reference. Plus, whenever you're in the mood to just sing along and have some fun, play the bonus Music CD.

If you have ever wanted to learn Spanish but thought that you didn't have the time, ***Drive & Learn*** is perfect for you!

Acknowledgments

I am grateful to the many talented individuals who have helped to bring *Drive & Learn Spanish* to the world. At Berlitz: Sheryl Olinsky Borg, my dream editor, for her enthusiastic support—linguistic, pedagogical, inspirational, and editorial; and Juergen Lorenz, for his attention to detail and hours of translation arbitration. For Heartworks International: Tru Doty, for his incredible orchestrations; James Rodriguez, for his pre-production assistance; Yolanda Helena Parilli, Senior Spanish Consultant, for her language expertise and great appreciation of the miraculous; Jack Walker for his audio expertise and phone support, both technical and personal; and Linda Beckerman, who knows where I am and is where I am wherever I am. Kudos to the glorious voices of the *Drive & Learn Spanish* cast Cándido González, Marenne Kashkin, Jim Brannigan, Letty Fores, José O. Molina, Ruth Iguiniz, Guylaine Laperrière, Michel Chevalier, Jack Walker, Teresa Labarga, Cathy Bolz, Amy Raupp, Paul Ehlers, Linda Beckerman, Josh Beckerman, and Bri Beckerman. Bri also deserves an extra hug of appreciation for her remarkable translation insights and proofreading talents. Thank you all for this joyous collaborative experience—and for your commitment to the art of entertainment in education.

Howard Beckerman
Stony Brook, NY
March 2000

This is Drive & Learn Spanish! Language-learning entertainment for people on the go!

 # Show

Getting Started

AT A HEALTH CLUB.

Jon:	One! Two! Three! Four! Five! Six! Boy, am I out of shape.
Elena:	¡Uno! ¡Dos! ¡Tres! ¡Cuatro! ¡Cinco! ¡Seis!
Jon:	Hi! I'm Jon.
Elena:	Hola.
Jon:	Oh. You speak Spanish.
Elena:	Sí. Yes. Español. Spanish.
Jon:	Oh. My Spanish is not very good. My name is Jon. Uh…me llamo Jon.
Elena:	Ah. Mucho gusto. Me llamo Elena.
Jon:	Oh, it's nice to meet you, Elena.
Elena:	¡El gusto es mío!

One, two, three, four,
five, six, seven, eight,
nine, ten.

Uno, dos, tres, cuatro,
cinco, seis, siete, ocho,
nueve, diez.

Hi.
It's nice to meet you.
It's nice to meet you, too.

Hola.
Mucho gusto.
El gusto es mío.

> **Mucho gusto.**
> It's nice to meet you.
> **El gusto es mío.**
> It's nice to meet you, too.

Jon: Hey, *I* can learn Spanish this way.

one	uno	uno
two	dos	dos
three	tres	tres
four	cuatro	cuatro
five	cinco	cinco
six	seis	seis
seven	siete	siete
eight	ocho	ocho
nine	nueve	nueve
ten	diez	diez
Hi.	Hola.	Hola.
It's nice to meet you.	Mucho gusto.	Mucho gusto.
It's nice to meet you, too.	El gusto es mío.	El gusto es mío.

> **Mucho gusto.**
> It's nice to meet you.
> **El gusto es mío.**
> It's nice to meet you, too.

Now you try it. Repeat the words in Spanish.

one	uno
two	dos
three	tres

four	**cuatro**
five	**cinco**
six	**seis**
seven	**siete**
eight	**ocho**
nine	**nueve**
ten	**diez**
Hi.	**Hola.**
It's nice to meet you.	**Mucho gusto.**
It's nice to meet you, too.	**El gusto es mío.**

Mucho gusto.
It's nice to meet you.
El gusto es mío.
It's nice to meet you, too.

Jon: Elena…would you like to…uh…I mean….
Maybe you could….
Elena: Yes, Jon?
Jon: What I'm trying to say is…maybe you can help
me learn some Spanish.
Elena: ¡Claro! Of course!

AT A SNACK BAR.

Jon: Something to drink?
Elena: Gracias. Thank you.
Jon: You're welcome.
Elena: De nada.
Jon: Oh, right. You're welcome is…de nada.
Elena: Muy bien. Very good.
Jon: Your English is much better than my Spanish.

Elena:	Muchas gracias.
Jon:	I know that means "Thank you very much."
Elena:	Muy bien.
Jon:	So, where are you from, Elena?
Elena:	I am from Peru. ¿De dónde es usted?
Jon:	Oh…me? I'm from New York. Uh…Nueva York.
Elena:	Soy de….
Jon:	Oh. Soy de Nueva York. I think I need a lot of practice!
Elena:	OK!

And you can practice, too. Repeat the Spanish.

Thank you.	**Gracias.**
You're welcome.	**De nada.**
Very good.	**Muy bien.**
Thank you very much.	**Muchas gracias.**
Where are you from?	**¿De dónde es usted?**
I'm from….	**Soy de….**

☞ *Now answer her question—and tell the truth!*

¿De dónde es usted?

_____

Now let's start a new day with our friend Jon, who's about to wake up to a big surprise.

IN JON'S BEDROOM. THE ALARM CLOCK RINGS.

| Jon: | Oh, no. I was having such a beautiful dream. What time is it? |

Sr. González:	¿Qué hora es?
Jon:	Excuse me?
Sr. González:	¿Perdón?
Jon:	What's going on here?
Sr. González:	I am the voice of your favorite Spanish teacher.
Jon:	Señor González? Is that really you? Yeah, that's you. You know, this is really perfect timing because I just met this Peruvian girl and I want to be able to talk to her in Spanish and—
Sr. González:	I know! That's why I'm here. And I'll stay with you all day. And soon, you'll be speaking Spanish in your dreams!
Jon:	Oh, I've got to get up and get ready for work. It's six o'clock!
Sr. González:	Son las seis. Don't you remember how to tell time?
Jon:	Oh, yeah. Son las seis.

Repeat the Spanish.

What time is it?	¿Qué hora es?
It's one o'clock.	Es la una.
It's two o'clock.	Son las dos.
It's three o'clock.	Son las tres.
It's four o'clock.	Son las cuatro.
It's five o'clock.	Son las cinco.
It's six o'clock.	Son las seis.
It's seven o'clock.	Son las siete.
It's eight o'clock.	Son las ocho.
It's nine o'clock.	Son las nueve.
It's ten o'clock.	Son las diez.
It's eleven o'clock.	Son las once.
It's twelve o'clock.	Son las doce.

☞ Now count the chimes and tell the time in Spanish. And then Señor González will say it after you.

¿Qué hora es?	Son las tres.

So, did you get the right answer? Let's try some more.

¿Qué hora es?	<u>Es la una.</u>
¿Qué hora es?	<u>Son las dos.</u>
¿Qué hora es?	<u>Son las cuatro.</u>
¿Qué hora es?	<u>Son las seis.</u>

IN THE BATHROOM.

Jon:	Oh, I'm really running late. I'd better get ready! Where's the soap?
Sr. González:	¿Dónde está el jabón?
Jon:	Oh, it's here!
Sr. González:	Está aquí.
Jon:	Now, where's the toothpaste?
Sr. González:	¿Dónde está la pasta de dientes?
Jon:	Oh! It's over there.
Sr. González:	Está allí.

> Where is it?
> ¿Dónde está?
> It's here!
> ¡Está aquí!
> Where is it?
> ¿Dónde está?
> It's there!
> ¡Está allí!
> ¿Dónde está?
> ¿Dónde está?
> ¿Dónde está?
> ¡Está aquí!
> ¡Está allí!
> ¡Está aquí!
> ¡Está allí!

Just listen.

the soap	el jabón
the towel	la toalla
the comb	el peine
the brush	el cepillo
the toothbrush	el cepillo de dientes
the toothpaste	la pasta de dientes
the shampoo	el champú

♪ Where is it?
¿Dónde está?
It's here!
¡Está aquí!
Where is it?
¿Dónde está?
It's there!
¡Está allí!
¿Dónde está?
¿Dónde está?
¿Dónde está?
¡Está aquí!
¡Está allí!
¡Está aquí!
¡Está allí!

Repeat after Señor González.

the soap	el jabón
the towel	la toalla
the comb	el peine
the brush	el cepillo
the toothbrush	el cepillo de dientes
the toothpaste	la pasta de dientes
the shampoo	el champú

♪ Where is it?
♪ ¿Dónde está?
♪ It's here!
♪ ¡Está aquí!
♪ Where is it
♪ ¿Dónde está?
♪ It's there!
♪ ¡Está allí!
♪ ¿Dónde está?
♪ ¿Dónde está?
♪ ¿Dónde está?
♪ ¡Está aquí!
♪ ¡Está allí!
♪ ¡Está aquí!
♪ ¡Está allí!

☞ *Now ask where the things are.*

el champú	¿Dónde está el champú?
la toalla	¿Dónde está la toalla?
el jabón	¿Dónde está el jabón?
el cepillo	¿Dónde está el cepillo?
el cepillo de dientes	¿Dónde está el cepillo de dientes?

Jon: Boy, that's a mouthful!

Where is it?

¿Dónde está?

It's here!

¡Está aquí!

Where is it?

¿Dónde está?

It's there!

¡Está allí!

¿Dónde está?

¿Dónde está?

¿Dónde está?

¿Dónde está?

¡Está aquí!

¡Está allí!

¡Está aquí!

¡Está allí!

Show ②

Ready to Leave

Jon:	Now what should I wear? Maybe something bright and cheery…something yellow.
Sr. González:	Amarillo.
Jon:	Yeah, amarillo. Yellow. Or something dramatic. Black!
Sr. González:	Negro.
Jon:	Or red!
Sr. González:	¡Rojo!
Jon:	Or blue.
Sr. González:	Azul.

Look at the colors of my life.
Mira los colores de mi vida.
Los colores de mi vida…
the colors of my life.

Now repeat the colors in Spanish.

red	rojo
yellow	amarillo
black	negro
white	blanco
orange	anaranjado

purple	morado
pink	rosado
blue	azul
green	verde
gray	gris
brown	marrón
beige	beige

> Look at the colors of my life.
> Mira los colores de mi vida.
> Los colores de mi vida...
> the colors of my life.

And what are you going to wear today?
Repeat the Spanish words.

a suit	un traje
a shirt	una camisa
pants	unos pantalones
a tie	una corbata
shoes	unos zapatos
a hat	un sombrero
a skirt	una falda
a dress	un vestido

> Look at the colors of my life.
> Mira los colores de mi vida.
> Los colores de mi vida...
> the colors of my life.

What color clothes are you going to wear?
Now repeat the Spanish phrases.

a blue suit	un traje azul
a white shirt	una camisa blanca
black pants	unos pantalones negros
a purple tie	una corbata morada
a red skirt	una falda roja
brown shoes	unos zapatos marrones

Look at the colors of my life.
Mira los colores de mi vida.
Los colores de mi vida...
the colors of my life.

Jon: All right! A white shirt, black pants, and for a little excitement—a purple and orange tie!

Sr. González: Purple and orange!?

Jon: ¡Sí! ¡Morado y anaranjado!

Sr. González: ¡Ah! ¡Muy bien!

IN THE KITCHEN.

Jon: I've got a big day ahead of me, so I'd better grab some breakfast. Toast.

Sr. González: Pan tostado.

Jon: Butter.

Sr. González: Mantequilla

Jon: Or maybe some rolls.

Sr. González: Bollitos de pan.

Jon: Jam.

Sr. González: Mermelada.

Jon:	Eggs.
Sr. González:	Huevos.
Jon:	Scrambled or fried?
Sr. González:	¿Revueltos o fritos?
Jon:	Scrambled eggs!
Sr. González:	Huevos revueltos.
Jon:	Juice.
Sr. González:	Jugo.
Jon:	Orange juice.
Sr. González:	Jugo de naranja.
Jon:	Coffee.
Sr. González:	Café.
Jon:	Or maybe tea.
Sr. González:	Té.

Are you hungry?
¿Tiene hambre?
Are you thirsty?
¿Tiene sed?
I'm hungry.
Tengo hambre.
I'm thirsty.
Tengo sed.
Enjoy your meal.
Buen provecho.
Buen provecho.
Enjoy your meal.

Repeat the Spanish.

toast	pan tostado
butter	mantequilla
rolls	bollitos de pan

jam	mermelada
eggs	huevos
scrambled or fried	revueltos o fritos
scrambled eggs	huevos revueltos
juice	jugo
orange juice	jugo de naranja
coffee	café
tea	té

Are you hungry?
¿Tiene hambre?
Are you thirsty?
¿Tiene sed?
I'm hungry.
Tengo hambre.
I'm thirsty.
Tengo sed.
Enjoy your meal.
Buen provecho.
Buen provecho.
Enjoy your meal.

Jon: OK! I've got to get out of here and get to the office!

OUTSIDE.

Jon: Oh, good. It's sunny.
Sr. González: Hace sol.
Jon: It's warm.
Sr. González: Hace calor.
Jon: Oh! What's happening?
Sr. González: ¿Qué pasa?
Jon: Yeah. ¿Qué pasa? What's happening? All of a sudden, it's windy!

Sr. González:	Hace viento.
Jon:	Did *you* do this, Señor González?
Sr. González:	What are you talking about? I'm just a Spanish teacher.
Jon:	It's raining!
Sr. González:	Está lloviendo.
Jon:	And it's cold.
Sr. González:	Hace frío.
Jon:	Oh, great. It's snowing.
Sr. González:	Está nevando.
Jon:	I can see this is going to be quite a day!

How's the weather?
¿Qué tiempo hace?
How's the weather?
¿Qué tiempo hace?
How's the weather...
¿Qué tiempo hace...
hoy?
today?
¡Hoy!
Today!
The weather is nice.
Hace buen tiempo.
The weather is bad.
Hace mal tiempo.
¡Hoy!
Today!
¡Hoy!
Today!

Repeat the weather expressions in Spanish.

It's warm.	Hace calor.
It's cold.	Hace frío.
It's sunny.	Hace sol.
It's windy.	Hace viento.
It's cloudy.	Está nublado.
It's raining.	Está lloviendo.
It's snowing.	Está nevando.

How's the weather?
¿Qué tiempo hace?
How's the weather?
¿Qué tiempo hace?
How's the weather...
¿Qué tiempo hace...
hoy?
today?
¡Hoy!
Today!
The weather is nice.
Hace buen tiempo.
The weather is bad.
Hace mal tiempo.
¡Hoy!
Today!
¡Hoy!
Today!

☞ *Now listen to the sounds, and then try to answer the question.*

¿Qué tiempo hace?	**Está lloviendo.**
¿Qué tiempo hace?	**Hace viento.**

THE CAR WON'T START.

Jon: Oh, no. Tell me it isn't true. Well, I refuse to get upset. This is only a test. And I'm going to stay calm. I'll just go by train.

By train.	En tren.
By bus.	En autobús.
By car.	En carro.
By bicycle.	En bicicleta.
By motorcycle.	En motocicleta.
By taxi.	En taxi.
By boat.	En bote.
By plane.	Por avión.
On foot.	A pie.

¿Cómo se llega allá?
¿Cómo se llega allá?
How do I get there?
How do I get there?
¿Cómo se llega allá?

Now repeat the modes of transportation in Spanish.

By train.	En tren.
By bus.	En autobús.

By car.	En carro.
By bicycle.	En bicicleta.
By motorcycle.	En motocicleta.
By taxi.	En taxi.
By boat.	En bote.
By plane.	Por avión.
On foot.	A pie.

¿Cómo se llega allá?
¿Cómo se llega allá?
How do I get there?
How do I get there?
¿Cómo se llega allá?

☞ Now listen to the sound to answer Señor González's question.

¿Cómo se llega allá?	En tren.
¿Cómo se llega allá?	En bote.
¿Cómo se llega allá?	A pie.
¿Cómo se llega allá?	Por avión.

¿Cómo se llega allá?
¿Cómo se llega allá?
How do I get there?
How do I get there?
¿Cómo se llega allá?

Show ③

On the Street

Jon: OK, so I'll take the train to work.
Sr. González: And I'll be helping you stay on track!

I'd like one ticket, please.
Quisiera un boleto, por favor.
I'd like...
Quisiera...
one ticket...
un boleto...
please.
por favor.

Now you say it. But let's build up to it from the end. Repeat.

---

por favor
un boleto, por favor
Quisiera un boleto, por favor.

I'd like one ticket, please.
Quisiera un boleto, por favor.

Let's go!
¡Vámonos!
It's getting late!
¡Se hace tarde!
Let's go!
¡Vámonos!
Hurry up!
¡Apurémosnos!

One way or round trip?	¿De ida? o ¿de ida y vuelta?
Round trip, please.	De ida y vuelta, por favor.
How much is that?	¿Cuánto cuesta?

Now repeat the Spanish.

one way	de ida
round trip	de ida y vuelta
One way or round trip?	¿De ida? o ¿de ida y vuelta?
Round trip, please.	De ida y vuelta, por favor.
How much is that?	¿Cuánto cuesta?

Let's go!
¡Vámonos!
It's getting late!
¡Se hace tarde!
Let's go!
¡Vámonos!
Hurry up!
¡Apurémosnos!

What time is the next train?
¿A qué hora sale el próximo tren?

Now repeat.

¿A qué hora…
sale el próximo tren?
¿A qué hora sale el próximo tren?

What time is the next train?
¿A qué hora sale el próximo tren?

the first train	el primer tren
the last train	el último tren
What time is the first train?	¿A qué hora sale el primer tren?
What time is the last train?	¿A qué hora sale el último tren?

Let's go!
¡Vámonos!
It's getting late!
¡Se hace tarde!
Let's go!
¡Vámonos!
Hurry up!
¡Apurémosnos!

What time is the next train?
¿A qué hora sale el próximo tren?

Repeat the times in Spanish.

At seven o'clock.	A las siete.
At ten after seven.	A las siete y diez.
At seven-fifteen.	A las siete y cuarto.
At seven-twenty.	A las siete y veinte.
At seven-thirty.	A las siete y media.
At twenty to eight.	A las ocho menos veinte.
At a quarter to eight.	A las ocho menos cuarto.

IN THE CITY.

Jon:	Two blocks from the office—with five minutes to spare. Maybe this'll be a good day after all.
Elena:	¡Buenos días, Jon!
Jon:	Elena, hello! I can't believe it! How *are* you? ¿Cómo está?
Elena:	I'm fine. Muy bien, gracias, ¿y usted?
Jon:	Oh, pretty good.
Sr. González:	Bastante bien.
Jon:	Bastante bien.
Elena:	Jon, I'd like you to meet my friend Luis. Quisiera presentarle a mi amigo Luis. Luis, este es Jon. Jon is learning Spanish.
Jon:	Mucho gusto.
Luis:	El gusto es mío, Jon. I'd love to stay and talk, but I have an appointment and I've really got to run.
Jon:	A pleasure meeting you.
Sr. González:	Un placer conocerle.
Jon:	Un placer conocerle.
Luis:	Igualmente. Same here. ¡Hasta luego!
Jon:	Bye!
Elena:	¡Chao, Luis!

Jon:	Well, unfortunately, I've got to get to the office—so….
Sr. González:	Invite her to lunch, invite her to lunch! ¿Le gustaría almorzar conmigo?
Jon:	Elena…¿le gustaría almorzar conmigo?
Elena:	Sí. ¡Me encantaría! I'd love to.
Sr. González:	Suggest 12 o'clock at the Downtown Café. ¿Qué le parece al mediodía en el Café del Centro?
Jon:	Uh…
Sr. González:	¿Qué le parece…
Jon:	¿Qué le parece…
Sr. González:	al mediodía
Jon:	al mediodía
Sr. González:	en el Café del Centro?
Jon:	en el Café del Centro?
Elena:	¡Perfecto! Jon, you're learning fast! Bueno, chao. ¡Nos vemos! See you later!
Jon:	¡Hasta luego!

♪ Good-bye!
♪ ¡Adiós!
♪ So long!
♪ ¡Chao!
♪ See you soon!
♪ ¡Nos vemos!
♪ ¡Nos vemos!
♪ See you later!
♪ ¡Hasta luego!
𝄢 See you later!

Repeat the Spanish phrases.

Good morning!	¡Buenos días!
Good afternoon!	¡Buenas tardes!
Good evening!	¡Buenas noches!
Good night!	¡Buenas noches!
How are you?	¿Cómo está?
Fine thanks, and you?	Bien, gracias, ¿y usted?
Pretty good.	Bastante bien.

Good-bye!
¡Adiós!
So long!
¡Chao!
See you soon!
¡Nos vemos!
¡Nos vemos!
See you later!
¡Hasta luego!
See you later!

I'd like you to meet my friend.	Quisiera presentarle a mi amigo.
This is my friend.	Éste es mi amigo.
It was a pleasure meeting you.	Un placer conocerle.
Same here.	Igualmente.

♪ Good-bye!	
♪ ¡Adiós!	
♪ So long!	
♪ ¡Chao!	
♪ See you soon!	
♪ ¡Nos vemos!	
♪ ¡Nos vemos!	
♪ See you later!	
♪ ¡Hasta luego!	
♪ See you later!	

Would you like to have lunch with me?	¿Le gustaría almorzar conmigo?
Would you like to have dinner with me?	¿Le gustaría cenar conmigo?
Would you like to have breakfast with me?	¿Le gustaría desayunar conmigo?
I'd love to!	¡Me encantaría!
How about...	¿Qué le parece...
at noon	al mediodía
at the Downtown Café?	en el Café del Centro?
How about noon at the Downtown Café?	¿Qué le parece al mediodía en el Café del Centro?

Good-bye!
¡Adiós!
So long!
¡Chao!
See you soon!
¡Nos vemos!
¡Nos vemos!
See you later!
¡Hasta luego!
See you later!

Show ④

At Work

AT THE OFFICE. JON SPEAKS TO HIS ASSISTANT.

Lynn: Good morning, Jon.

Jon: Good morning, Lynn. What's on the schedule today?

Lynn: You have an appointment at ten and another one at eleven.

Jon: Then I have a lunch appointment at twelve.

Lynn: There's also a staff meeting this afternoon at three.

Jon: And we have to finish that new project proposal by Friday.

Lynn: We're going to be really busy!

Busy?	¿Ocupado?
Always!	¡Siempre!
Free time?	¿Tiempo libre?
Never!	¡Nunca!
And sometimes…	Y a veces…
I don't have time to think…	no tengo tiempo para pensar…
or time to breathe.	ni tiempo para respirar.

¿Ocupado?
¡Siempre!
¿Tiempo libre?
¡Nunca!
Y a veces,
no tengo tiempo para pensar
ni tiempo para respirar.

Repeat the Spanish words.

a day	un día
a week	una semana
a month	un mes
a year	un año
a season	una estación
a schedule	un horario
an appointment	una cita
a meeting	una reunión
the staff	el personal
a project	un proyecto
a proposal	una propuesta
busy	ocupado
free time	tiempo libre
always	siempre
sometimes	a veces
never	nunca

¿Ocupado?
¡Siempre!
¿Tiempo libre?
¡Nunca!
Y a veces,
no tengo tiempo para pensar
ni tiempo para respirar.

Repeat the days of the week in Spanish.

Monday	lunes
Tuesday	martes
Wednesday	miércoles
Thursday	jueves

Friday	viernes
Saturday	sábado
Sunday	domingo

> ¿Ocupada?
> ¡Siempre!
> ¿Tiempo libre?
> ¡Nunca!
> Y a veces,
> no tengo tiempo para pensar
> ni tiempo para respirar.

Repeat the months of the year in Spanish.

January	enero
February	febrero
March	marzo
April	abril
May	mayo
June	junio
July	julio
August	agosto
September	septiembre
October	octubre
November	noviembre
December	diciembre

```
¿Ocupado?
¡Siempre!
¿Tiempo libre?
¡Nunca!
Y a veces,
no tengo tiempo para pensar
ni tiempo para respirar.
```

Repeat the seasons in Spanish.

winter	el invierno
spring	la primavera
summer	el verano
fall	el otoño

```
¿Ocupado?
¡Siempre!
¿Tiempo libre?
¡Nunca!
Y a veces,
no tengo tiempo para pensar
ni tiempo para respirar.
```

So what do you do with your time? What do you do for a living?

What do you do?	
¿Qué hace usted?	
¿Qué haces tú?	
What do you do?	
What do you do?	
¿Qué hace usted?	
¿Qué haces tú?	
What do you do?	

Repeat the sentences in Spanish—after the man or after the woman.

I'm an accountant.	**Soy contador.**
	Soy contadora.
I'm a lawyer.	**Soy abogado.**
	Soy abogada.
I'm a doctor.	**Soy médico.**
	Soy médico.
I'm a computer programmer.	**Soy programador de sistemas.**
	Soy programadora de sistemas.

What do you do?	
¿Qué hace usted?	
¿Qué haces tú?	
What do you do?	

I'm a businessperson.	Soy hombre de negocios.
	Soy mujer de negocios.
I'm a salesperson.	Soy vendedor.
	Soy vendedora.
I'm a cashier.	Soy cajero.
	Soy cajera.
I'm an engineer.	Soy ingeniero.
	Soy ingeniera.

What do you do?
¿Qué hace usted?
¿Qué haces tú?
What do you do?

I'm a secretary.	Soy secretario.
	Soy secretaria.
I'm an actor.	Soy actor.
	Soy actriz.
I'm a student.	Soy estudiante.
	Soy estudiante.
I'm a teacher.	Soy maestro.
	Soy maestra.

What do you do?
¿Qué hace usted?
¿Qué haces tú?
What do you do?

Jon: Can I borrow your dictionary, please?
Lynn: Of course.
Jon: And can I use the stapler?

Lynn:	Sure. It's in the drawer.
Jon:	Oh, and could you get me that file for the staff meeting?
Lynn:	No problem.

Yes, of course!
Sí, ¡cómo no!
¡Por supuesto!
¡Cómo no!
Yes! Sure!
¡Sí! ¡Claro!
¡Por supuesto!
¡Cómo no!

Repeat these office items in Spanish.

the dictionary	el diccionario
the pen	el bolígrafo
the pencil	el lápiz
the desk	el escritorio
the drawer	la gaveta
the chair	la silla
the book	el libro

Can I borrow your pen, please?
¿Me presta su bolígrafo, por favor?
Can I borrow...
¿Me presta...
your pen...
su bolígrafo...
please?
por favor?

Now you say it, phrase by phrase from the end. Repeat.

---

por favor
su bolígrafo, por favor
¿Me presta su bolígrafo, por favor?

Yes, of course!
Sí, ¡cómo no!
¡Por supuesto!
¡Cómo no!
Yes! Sure!
¡Sí! ¡Claro!
¡Por supuesto!
¡Cómo no!

Now ask to borrow some other things.

your dictionary	su diccionario
	¿Me presta su diccionario?
your pencil	su lápiz
	¿Me presta su lápiz?
your desk	su escritorio
	¿Me presta su escritorio?
your chair	su silla
	¿Me presta su silla?

Yes, of course!
Sí, ¡cómo no!
¡Por supuesto!
¡Cómo no!
Yes! Sure!
¡Sí! ¡Claro!
¡Por supuesto!
¡Cómo no!

Now here are some other office items. Repeat the Spanish.

the notebook	el cuaderno
the telephone	el teléfono
the computer	la computadora
the file	el documento
the folder	la carpeta
the file cabinet	el archivador
the stapler	la engrapadora

Jon:	Hmm…where's the file?
Sr. González:	¿Dónde está el documento?
Jon:	Oh, it's on the desk.
Sr. González:	Está *sobre* el escritorio.
Jon:	And the notebook?
Sr. González:	el cuaderno
Jon:	In the drawer.
Sr. González:	*Adentro* de la gaveta.
Jon:	Where's the folder?
Sr. González:	¿Dónde está la carpeta?
Jon:	Under the book.
Sr. González:	*Debajo* del libro.

On, in, under!
¡Sobre, adentro, debajo!
On, in, under!
¡Sobre, adentro, debajo!

Now repeat these locations in Spanish.

on the desk	sobre el escritorio
in the drawer	adentro de la gaveta
under the notebook	debajo del cuaderno
on the book	sobre el libro
in the file folder	adentro de la carpeta
under the chair	debajo de la silla

On, in, under!
¡Sobre, adentro, debajo!
On, in, under!
¡Sobre, adentro, debajo!

the file	el documento
the folder	la carpeta
The file is in the folder.	El documento está adentro de la carpeta.

☞ *Now try to say the location before Señor González says it.*

the notebook	el cuaderno
the desk	el escritorio
The notebook is on the desk.	El cuaderno está sobre el escritorio.
the dictionary	el diccionario
the chair	la silla
The dictionary is under the chair.	El diccionario está debajo de la silla.

On, in, under!
¡Sobre, adentro, debajo!
On, in, under!
¡Sobre, adentro, debajo!
On, in, under!
¡Sobre, adentro, debajo!
On, in, under!
¡Sobre, adentro, debajo!

Show ⑤

Lunch Hour

IN A RESTAURANT.

Jon: A table for two, please.

Hostess: Right this way.

Elena: Could we have the table by the window?

Hostess: Certainly. And your waiter will be right with you.

Elena: Thank you.

Jon: Elena, it's so amazing that we ran into each other on the street this morning.

Elena: A great coincidence.

Jon: Or destiny.

Una mesa para dos.
A table for two.
Una mesa para dos.
A table for two.
We have a reservation, una reservación.
This is our song, nuestra canción.
Una mesa para dos.
A table for two.
Una mesa para dos.
A table for two.

Repeat these words in Spanish.

a fork	un tenedor
a knife	un cuchillo
a spoon	una cuchara
a napkin	una servilleta
a glass	un vaso
a cup	una taza
a plate	un plato

Una mesa para dos.
A table for two.
Una mesa para dos.
A table for two.
We have a reservation, una reservación.
This is our song, nuestra canción.
Una mesa para dos.
A table for two.
Una mesa para dos.
A table for two.

Now let's look at the menu. Repeat the words in Spanish.

appetizers	entradas
soup	sopas
fish	pescados
seafood	mariscos
meat	carnes
vegetables	vegetales
salads	ensaladas
fruit	frutas
cheese	quesos
desserts	postres
drinks	bebidas

♪ Una mesa para dos.
A table for two.
Una mesa para dos.
A table for two.
We have a reservation, una reservación.
This is our song, nuestra canción.
Una mesa para dos.
A table for two.
Una mesa para dos.
A table for two.

Jon: So what are you in the mood for, Elena?
Elena: Hmm…well…I think I'll just have a salad and some mineral water. How about you? ¿Y usted? Or maybe now that we know each other a little better, I can say, "¿Y tú?" And you? What would you like? ¿Qué quieres?
Jon: Well…tengo mucha hambre. I'm really hungry. I'm going to have the special vegetable soup… and a steak with fries. And maybe a glass of red wine.

♪ Una mesa para dos.
A table for two.
Una mesa para dos.
A table for two.
We have a reservation, una reservación.
This is our song, nuestra canción.
Una mesa para dos.
A table for two.
Una mesa para dos.
A table for two.

Repeat these menu items in Spanish.

vegetable soup	una sopa de verduras
a hamburger	una hamburguesa
French fries	papas fritas
a salad	una ensalada
a sandwich	un sándwich
a steak	un bistec
shrimp	camarones
rice with chicken	arroz con pollo
vanilla ice cream	helado de vainilla
chocolate cake	torta de chocolate
coffee	café
tea	té
a bottle of mineral water	una botella de agua mineral
a glass of wine	una copa de vino
a beer	una cerveza

Una mesa para dos.
A table for two.
Una mesa para dos.
A table for two.
We have a reservation, una reservación.
This is our song, nuestra canción.
Una mesa para dos.
A table for two.
Una mesa para dos.
A table for two.

Jon: Well, now I think we're ready...uh...to order.
Waiter!

♪ ¡Camarero! ¡Camarero!
Are you ready to order?
♪ ¿Quisiera ordenar?
♪ ¡Camarero! ¡Camarero!
Are you ready to order?
♪ ¿Quisiera ordenar?
♪ What would you like to drink?
♪ ¿Qué desearía tomar?
What would you like to order?
♪ ¿Qué le gustaría ordenar?
♪ I'll have…
♪ Quisiera…
I'd like…
♪ Me gustaría…

Now order from the menu. Repeat the Spanish.

a salad	una ensalada
I'll have a salad.	Quisiera una ensalada.
a hamburger	una hamburguesa
I'll have a hamburger.	Quisiera una hamburguesa.
French fries	papas fritas
I'd like French fries.	Me gustarían papas fritas.
a beer	una cerveza
I'd like a beer.	Me gustaría una cerveza.

♪ I'll have…
♪ Quisiera…
♪ I'd like…
♪ Me gustaría…

*☞ Now try to order each of these items—before you
hear two ways to give the order.*

a salad	**Quisiera una ensalada.**
	Me gustaría una ensalada.
a hamburger	**Quisiera una hamburguesa.**
	Me gustaría una hamburguesa.
French fries	**Quisiera papas fritas.**
	Me gustarían papas fritas.
vegetable soup	**Quisiera sopa de verduras.**
	Me gustaría sopa de verduras.
a bottle of mineral water	**Quisiera una botella de agua mineral.**
	Me gustaría una botella de agua mineral.
a glass of wine	**Quisiera una copa de vino.**
	Me gustaría una copa de vino.

I'll have…
Quisiera…
I'd like…
Me gustaría…
¡Camarero! ¡Camarero!
Are you ready to order?
¿Quisiera ordenar?
¡Camarero! ¡Camarero!
Are you ready to order?
¿Quisiera ordenar?

♪ What would you like to drink?
♪ ¿Qué desearía tomar?
♪ What would you like to order?
♪ ¿Qué le gustaría ordenar?
♪ I'll have…
♪ Quisiera…
♪ I'd like…
♪ Me gustaría…
♪ ¡Camarero! ¡Camarero!
♪ Are you ready to order?
♪ ¿Quisiera ordenar?
♪ ¡Camarero! ¡Camarero!
♪ Are you ready to order?
♪ ¿Quisiera ordenar?
♪ What would you like to drink?
♪ ¿Qué desearía tomar?
♪ What would you like to order?
♪ ¿Qué le gustaría ordenar?
♪ I'll have…
♪ Quisiera…
♪ I'd like…
𝄢 Me gustaría…

Jon: The check, please.
Elena: La cuenta, por favor.

🎼 ¡La cuenta, por favor!
　 ¡La cuenta, por favor!
𝄢 ¡Camarero!

Show 6

On the Phone

BACK AT THE OFFICE.

Lynn: Hi, Jon. So...how was lunch?

Jon: Delicious...delicioso...deliciosa.

Lynn: I'm glad you enjoyed it. But while you were out it's been crazy here. There's a pile of messages for you on your desk.

Jon: Well, I'm ready for action!

Hello?	¿Aló?
May I help you?	A la orden.
Can I speak to Jonathan Simon, please?	¿Puedo hablar con Jonathan Simon, por favor?
Who's calling, please?	¿Quién llama, por favor?
This is Daniel Rodríguez.	Es Daniel Rodríguez.
Can you spell that, please?	¿Puede deletrearlo, por favor?
Daniel: D-A-N-I-E-L	D-A-N-I-E-L
Rodríguez: R-O-D-R-I-G-U-E-Z	R-O-D-R-I-G-U-E-Z
Hold on, please.	Un momento, por favor.
He can't come to the phone right now.	Él está ocupado en este momento.
Would you like to leave a message?	¿Desearía dejarle un mensaje?
Please ask him to call me.	Por favor, dígale que me llame.

What's your phone number?	¿Cuál es su número de teléfono?
Six-nine-eight… seven-three-four-two.	Seis-nueve-ocho… siete-tres-cuatro-dos.
Could you repeat that, please?	¿Podría repetirlo, por favor?
Six-nine-eight… seven-three-four-two.	Seis-nueve-ocho… siete-tres-cuatro-dos.
Thank you. I'll give him the message.	Gracias. Yo le daré su mensaje.
Thank you. Good-bye.	Gracias. Adiós.

Hold on, please.
Un momento, por favor.
Un momento, por favor.
Un momento, por favor.

He can't come to the phone now.
Él está ocupado
en este momento.
Él está ocupado.

She can't come to the phone now.
Ella está ocupada
en este momento.

Who's calling, please?
¿Quién llama, por favor?
¿Quién llama, por favor?
¿Quién llama, por favor?

Can you spell that, please?
¿Puede deletrearlo, por favor?
Por favor.

Could you repeat that, please?
¿Podría repetirlo, por favor?
Por favor?

Would you like to leave a message?
¿Desearía dejarle un mensaje?

Please ask him to call me.
Por favor, dígale que me llame.

Please ask her to call me.
Por favor, dígale que me llame.

I'll give him the message.
Yo le daré su mensaje.
Yo le daré su mensaje.

I'll give her the message.
Yo le daré su mensaje.
Yo le daré su mensaje.

Hold on, please.
Un momento, por favor.
Un momento, por favor.
Un momento, por favor.

Hold on, please.
Un momento, por favor.
Un momento, por favor.
Un momento, por favor.

Can I speak to Jonathan Simon, please?
¿Puedo hablar con Jonathan Simon, por favor?

Now ask to speak to these people. Repeat.

María Añez
¿Puedo hablar con María Añez, por favor?
Luis García
¿Puedo hablar con Luis García, por favor?
Carolina Hurtado
¿Puedo hablar con Carolina Hurtado, por favor?

Hold on, please.
Un momento, por favor.
Un momento, por favor.
Un momento, por favor.

Hold on, please.
Un momento, por favor.
Un momento, por favor.
Un momento, por favor.

Lynn:	Who's calling, please?
Carolina:	Carolina Hurtado.
Lynn:	Can you spell that, please?
Carolina:	*(in English)* Carolina: C-A-R-O-L-I-N-A. Hurtado: H-U-R-T-A-D-O.

¿Quién llama, por favor?
Carolina Hurtado.
¿Puede deletrearlo, por favor?
Carolina: *(in Spanish)* C-A-R-O-L-I-N-A.
Hurtado: *(in Spanish)* H-U-R-T-A-D-O.

(in Spanish) A-B-C-D-E-F-G
H-I-J-K-L-M-N-Ñ-O-P
Q-R-S-T-U-V
W-X-Y-Z

¿Quién llama, por favor?
Luis García
¿Puede deletrearlo, por favor?
Luis: *(in Spanish)* L-U-I-S
García: *(in Spanish)* G-A-R-C-I-A

(in Spanish) A-B-C-D-E-F-G
H-I-J-K-L-M-N-Ñ-O-P
Q-R-S-T-U-V
W-X-Y-Z
A-B-C-D-E-F-G
H-I-J-K-L-M-N-Ñ-O-P
Q-R-S-T-U-V
W-X-Y-Z
A-B-C-D-E-F-G
H-I-J-K-L-M-N-Ñ-O-P
Q-R-S-T-U-V
W-X-Y-Z

☞ Now you try to spell each name in Spanish after Jon
   spells it in English.

¿Quién llama, por favor?
Daniel Rodríguez
Daniel: D-A-N-I-E-L
(in Spanish) **D-A-N-I-E-L**
Rodríguez: R-O-D-R-I-G-U-E-Z
(in Spanish) **R-O-D-R-I-G-U-E-Z**

¿Quién llama, por favor?
Diana Peña
Diana: D-I-A-N-A
(in Spanish) **D-I-A-N-A**
Peña: P-E-Ñ-A
(in Spanish) **P-E-Ñ-A**

(in Spanish) **A-B-C-D-E-F-G**
H-I-J-K-L-M-N-Ñ-O-P
Q-R-S-T-U-V
W-X-Y-Z
A-B-C-D-E-F-G
H-I-J-K-L-M-N-Ñ-O-P
Q-R-S-T-U-V
W-X-Y-Z

¿Cuál es su número de teléfono?
What's your phone number?
¿Cuál es su número de teléfono?
What's your phone number?

(in English) **732-8491**
(in Spanish) **732-8491**

🎼 ¿Cuál es su número de teléfono?
What's your phone number?
🎵 ¿Cuál es su número de teléfono?
🎼 What's your phone number?

☞ *Now you say the numbers in Spanish.*

(in English) **651-9026**
(in Spanish) **651-9026**

🎼 ¿Cuál es su número de teléfono?
What's your phone number?
🎵 ¿Cuál es su número de teléfono?
🎼 What's your phone number?

(in English) **343-6112**
(in Spanish) **343-6112**

🎼 ¿Cuál es su número de teléfono?
What's your phone number?
🎵 ¿Cuál es su número de teléfono?
🎼 What's your phone number?

(in English) **888-5957**
(in Spanish) **888-5957**

♪ ¿Cuál es su número de teléfono?
What's your phone number?
♪ ¿Cuál es su número de teléfono?
What's your phone number?

(in English) **232-3223**
(in Spanish) **232-3223**

Lynn:	Jon, I have a call for you on line one.
Jon:	Thanks, Lynn. Hello?
Elena:	Hello, Jon.
Jon:	Elena. Hi!
Elena:	I just wanted to thank you again for lunch. I had a wonderful time.
Jon:	I did, too.
Sr. González:	Yo también.
Jon:	Yo también. We'll have to do it again.
Elena:	How about this weekend?
Jon:	Yeah.
Elena:	Listen, call me. Llámame. Tomorrow at work. Everyone in the office speaks Spanish. You can practice with the receptionist.
Jon:	I'm *ready* for them.
Elena:	My office number is 375-6219.
Jon:	Tres-siete-cinco…seis-dos-uno-nueve.
Elena:	That's it! ¡Eso es!

♪ ¿Cuál es su número de teléfono?
What's your phone number?
♪ ¿Cuál es su número de teléfono?
What's your phone number?

☞ *What's your phone number? Say it in Spanish!*

_____

Jon:	I'll call you tomorrow!
Sr. González:	Yo te llamaré mañana.
Jon:	Yo te llamaré mañana.
Elena:	¡Chao!
Jon:	Till tomorrow!
Sr. González:	¡Hasta mañana!
Jon:	¡Hasta mañana!

Show ⟨7⟩

Around the Neighborhood

ON THE STREET, OUTSIDE JON'S OFFICE BUILDING.

Lynn: Well, it was a good day, but I'm glad it's five o'clock.

Jon: Yo también. Uh—me, too.

Lynn: You're speaking a lot of Spanish lately. I guess you're motivated.

Jon: Es verdad. That's true. Anyway Lynn, I really did appreciate all your hard work today.

Lynn: That's what I'm here for. So what have you got planned for the evening?

Jon: Well, I'm going to my parents for dinner tonight, but I've got a whole list of chores to do first, and I'm not going to have time to go home. So I've got to find everything that I need around *here*.

Lynn: Oh, there's my bus! See you tomorrow, Jon!

Jon: Take care! ¡Cuídate! OK. Now…where do I go first? Maybe to the post office.

Sr. González: el correo

Jon: And then the bank.

Sr. González: el banco

Jon: And the florist.

Sr. González: la floristería

Repeat the Spanish.

the post office	el correo
the bank	el banco
the florist	la floristería
the library	la biblioteca
I'm looking for the post office.	Estoy buscando el correo.
I'm looking for the bank.	Estoy buscando el banco.
I'm looking for the florist.	Estoy buscando la floristería.
I'm looking for the library.	Estoy buscando la biblioteca.

Straight ahead!	¡Derecho!
On the left!	¡A la izquierda!
On the right!	¡A la derecha!
On the corner!	¡En la esquina!

Or maybe it's just around the corner!
¡O quizás está a la vuelta de la esquina!

Around the corner!
¡A la vuelta de la esquina!
Across the street!
¡Enfrente!
Turn left!
¡Doble a la izquierda!
Turn right!
¡Doble a la derecha!
It's very close—it's just around the corner!
Está muy cerca—¡a la vuelta de la esquina!

Repeat the Spanish.

the department store	el almacén
the bookstore	la librería
the gift shop	la tienda de regalos
the butcher shop	la carnicería
I'm looking for the department store.	Estoy buscando el almacén.
I'm looking for the bookstore.	Estoy buscando la librería.
I'm looking for the gift shop.	Estoy buscando la tienda de regalos.
I'm looking for the butcher shop.	Estoy buscando la carnicería.

Straight ahead!	¡Derecho!
On the left!	¡A la izquierda!
On the right!	¡A la derecha!
On the corner!	¡En la esquina!

Or maybe it's just around the corner!
¡O quizás está a la vuelta de la esquina!

Around the corner!
¡A la vuelta de la esquina!
Across the street!
¡Enfrente!
Turn left!
¡Doble a la izquierda!
Turn right!
¡Doble a la derecha!
It's very close—it's just around the corner!
Está muy cerca—¡a la vuelta de la esquina!

Repeat the Spanish.

the school	la escuela
the park	el parque
the hospital	el hospital
the police station	la estación de policía
Where's the nearest school?	¿Dónde está la escuela más cercana?
Where's the nearest park?	¿Dónde está el parque más cercano?
Where's the nearest hospital?	¿Dónde está el hospital más cercano?
Where's the nearest police station?	¿Dónde está la estación de policía más cercana?

Around the corner!	
¡A la vuelta de la esquina!	
Across the street!	
¡Enfrente!	
Turn left!	
¡Doble a la izquierda!	
Turn right!	
¡Doble a la derecha!	
It's very close—it's just around the corner!	
Está muy cerca—¡a la vuelta de la esquina!	

Repeat the Spanish.

the bakery	la panadería
the restaurant	el restaurante
the pharmacy	la farmacia
the supermarket	el supermercado
Where's the nearest bakery?	¿Dónde está la panadería más cercana?
Where's the nearest restaurant?	¿Dónde está el restaurante más cercano?
Where's the nearest pharmacy?	¿Dónde está la farmacia más cercana?
Where's the nearest supermarket?	¿Dónde está el supermercado más cercano?

Around the corner!	
¡A la vuelta de la esquina!	
Across the street!	
¡Enfrente!	
Turn left!	
¡Doble a la izquierda!	
Turn right!	
¡Doble a la derecha!	
It's very close—it's just around the corner!	
Está muy cerca—¡a la vuelta de la esquina!	

☞ Now…where should we go? Listen and say where, in Spanish.

I need to buy stamps.	Necesito comprar estampillas.
Let's go to the post office.	<u>Vamos al correo.</u>
I need to buy bread.	Necesito comprar pan.
Let's go to the bakery.	<u>Vamos a la panadería.</u>
I need to buy flowers.	Necesito comprar flores.
Let's go to the florist.	<u>Vamos a la floristería.</u>

How much is that?	
¿Cuánto cuesta?	
How much is that?	
¿Cuánto cuesta?	
That's expensive!	
¡Es caro!	
That's cheap!	
¡Es barato!	
That's all, thanks.	
Eso es todo, gracias.	
That's all!	

Find out how you can pay. Repeat the questions in Spanish.

Can I pay by check?	¿Puedo pagar con cheque?
Can I pay by credit card?	¿Puedo pagar con tarjeta de crédito?
Can I pay cash?	¿Puedo pagar en efectivo?
Of course!	¡No faltaba más!

☞ *Now once again, where should we go? Listen and say where, in Spanish.*

I need to buy a book.	Necesito comprar un libro.
Let's go to the bookstore.	<u>Vamos a la librería.</u>
I need to buy meat.	Necesito comprar carne.
Let's go to the butcher shop.	<u>Vamos a la carnicería.</u>
I need to buy a gift.	Necesito comprar un regalo.
Let's go to the gift shop.	<u>Vamos a la tienda de regalos.</u>

How much is that?
¿Cuánto cuesta?
How much is that?
¿Cuánto cuesta?
That's expensive!
¡Es caro!
That's cheap!
¡Es barato!
That's all, thanks.
Eso es todo, gracias.
That's all!

How much is that?
¿Cuánto cuesta?
How much is that?
¿Cuánto cuesta?
That's expensive!
¡Es caro!
That's cheap!
¡Es barato!
That's all, thanks.
Eso es todo, gracias.
That's all!
That's all!

Show 8

At Home

AT THE HOME OF JON'S PARENTS.

Mom: Jonathan, come in! Give me a hug!

Jon: So how's my favorite mother?

THE DOG APPROACHES.

Hey, Buddy! How are you, boy?

Mom: David! It's Jon! Melissa! Your brother's here!

Dad: Jon! You're looking good.

Jon: Hey, Dad.

Dad: So what's the latest?

Jon: Well, I'm teaching myself to speak Spanish.

Melissa: ¿Por qué?, Johnny? Why? Díme, ¿por qué? Tell me why.

Jon: Melissa! Buenas noches. Good evening, little sister. What color is your hair?

Melissa: Well, it's supposed to be blonde, but it turned purple somehow.

Jon: An interesting shade of *morado*. Always plenty of surprises when I come to visit.

Mom: Wait till you see the house. Come into the living room first!

Jon: Mom! What happened to the green couch?

Mom: We gave it to Aunt Karen. We decided it was time to redecorate.

Dad: And while we were re-doing the living room, your mother decided that every other room in the house needed a face-lift, too.

Mom: Come on, we'll give you a tour!

Welcome!
¡Bienvenido!
Welcome home!
¡Bienvenido a casa!
I'm so glad you're here!
¡Qué alegría que estás aquí!
¡Bienvenido!

Have a seat!
¡Siéntate!
Make yourself at home!
¡Siéntete en tu casa!
I'm so glad you came!
¡Qué bueno que viniste!
¡Qué bueno que viniste!
I'm so glad you came!

Welcome!
¡Bienvenido!
Welcome home!
¡Bienvenido a casa!
I'm so glad you're here!
¡Qué alegría que estás aquí!
¡Bienvenido!

Say the names of the rooms and other parts of the house in Spanish.

the living room	la sala
the kitchen	la cocina
the dining room	el comedor
the bedroom	el cuarto
the bathroom	el baño

the den	el estudio
the backyard	el patio
the garage	el garaje
the basement	el sótano
the attic	el ático
the window	la ventana

Mom: So what do you think of the living room, Jonathan? Look at what's new!

Repeat the words in Spanish.

the couch	el sofá
the armchair	el sillón
the rug	la alfombra
the bookcase	el estante de libros
the coffee table	la mesa de centro
the lamp	la lámpara
the painting	la pintura
the plant	la planta
the piano	el piano
the television	la televisión
the stereo	el equipo de sonido
the VCR	la video

Sr. González: Jon, say something nice to your mother.

Repeat the compliments in Spanish.

That's a nice couch!	¡Qué sofá tan lindo!
That's a nice armchair!	¡Qué sillón tan lindo!
That's a nice rug!	¡Qué alfombra tan linda!
That's a nice bookcase!	¡Qué estante de libros tan lindo!
That's a nice coffee table!	¡Qué mesa de centro tan linda!
That's a nice lamp!	¡Qué lámpara tan linda!
That's a nice painting!	¡Qué pintura tan linda!
That's a nice plant!	¡Qué planta tan linda!
That's a nice piano!	¡Qué piano tan lindo!
That's a nice television!	¡Qué televisión tan linda!
That's a nice stereo!	¡Qué equipo de sonido tan lindo!
That's a nice VCR!	¡Qué video tan linda!

Now accept a compliment in Spanish. Repeat.

So glad you like it!	¡Me encanta que te guste!
That's very nice of you to say!	¡Muy amable!
I'm glad you feel that way!	Me alegra que te sientas así.

So glad you like it!
That's very nice of you to say!
And I'm glad you feel that way!

¡Me encanta que te guste!
¡Muy amable!
Me alegra que te sientas así.

Welcome!
¡Bienvenido!
Welcome home!
¡Bienvenido a casa!
I'm so glad you're here!
¡Qué alegría que estás aquí!
¡Bienvenido!

Mom: Come look at the kitchen, Jon. It's very high-tech!

Say the names of these kitchen items. Repeat the Spanish.

the refrigerator	la nevera
the oven	el horno
the microwave oven	el horno microondas
the stove	la estufa
the sink	el fregadero
the dishwasher	el lavaplatos

Now ask if those things are new. Then repeat the Spanish.

Is that a new refrigerator?	¿Es esa una nevera nueva?
Is that a new oven?	¿Es eso un horno nuevo?
Is that a new microwave oven?	¿Es eso un horno microondas nuevo?
Is that a new stove?	¿Es esa una estufa nueva?
Is that a new sink?	¿Es eso un fregadero nuevo?
Is that a new dishwasher?	¿Es eso un lavaplatos nuevo?

Mom: Yes, it's all new, Jon! So what do you think?
Jon: It's all great. Enjoy it and use it well!

So glad you like it!
That's very nice of you to say!
And I'm glad you feel that way!

¡Me encanta que te guste!
¡Muy amable!
Me alegra que te sientas así.

Welcome!
¡Bienvenido!
Welcome home!
¡Bienvenido a casa!
I'm so glad you're here!
¡Qué alegría que estás aquí!
¡Bienvenido!

Jon: Mom, everything looks really wonderful. But I can't imagine what you've done to my old bedroom.

Mom: Come, I'll show you.

IN JON'S OLD ROOM.

Jon: Oh, Mom. I should have known better.

Mom: You didn't really think I'd change everything in our house, did you?

What's in the bedroom? Repeat the Spanish.

a bed	una cama
a pillow	una almohada
a blanket	una cobija
a closet	un closet
boxes	cajas
a dresser	una cómoda
a mirror	un espejo
a window	una ventana

En mi cuarto,
hay una cama.
Hay una almohada sobre la cama
y una cobija
en mi cuarto.
En mi cuarto.

In my room,
there's a bed.
And there's a pillow on the bed.
And there's a blanket on the bed
in my room.
In my room.

En mi cuarto,
hay un closet.
Y hay cajas en el closet
con mis fotos en las cajas
en mi cuarto.
En mi cuarto.

In my room,
there's a closet.
And there are boxes in the closet
with my photos in the boxes
in my room.
In my room.

I remember many days
and many nights right here.
In my room memories
suddenly appear.

Yo recuerdo muchos días
y tantas noches aquí.
Recuerdos en mi cuarto
vienen hacia mí.

En mi cuarto,
hay una cómoda.
Y hay un espejo sobre la cómoda
y una ventana cerca del espejo
en mi cuarto.
En mi cuarto.

In my room,
there's a dresser.
And there's a mirror by the dresser

and a window near the mirror
in my room.
In my room.

Through the window, I can see
the seasons change.
And in the mirror, I can see
something very strange.

A través de la ventana puedo ver
las estaciones cambiar.
Y en el espejo puedo ver
algo muy extraño pasar.
In the mirror, I can see
something very strange.

In my room,
there's a man...
there's a woman...
and a boy with the man,
and a girl with the woman,
in my room.
In my room.

En mi cuarto,
hay un hombre...
hay una mujer...
hay un niño con el hombre,
una niña con la mujer
en mi cuarto.
En mi cuarto.

Show 9

Family Time

THE DOORBELL RINGS.

Mom:	Come on in! The door is open!
Guests:	Hi! How are you? Nice to see you! You look terrific! Hello, Hello, Hello!
Mom:	Jonathan's here, and dinner's almost ready. So just make yourselves comfortable and I'll be right with you.
Jon:	Aunt Susan! Hi, Uncle Bill. It's great to see you.
Dawn:	Hi, Jon.
Jon:	Dawn? Is that really you?
Dawn:	I'm still your baby cousin!
Jon:	Well, I guess it's been longer than I realized. How old are you now?
Dawn:	Seventeen.
Jon:	Wow! It's amazing what a few years can do.

My family!
¡Mi familia!
This is my family.
Le presento a mi familia.
I'd like you to meet my family.
Me gustaría que conociera a mi familia.

Repeat the Spanish words.

my father	mi padre
my mother	mi madre
my sister	mi hermana
my brother	mi hermano
my husband	mi esposo
my wife	mi esposa
my son	mi hijo
my daughter	mi hija
my aunt	mi tía
my uncle	mi tío
my cousins	mis primos
my niece	mi sobrina
my nephew	mi sobrino
my grandfather	mi abuelo
my grandmother	mi abuela
my grandson	mi nieto
my granddaughter	mi nieta

My family!
¡Mi familia!
This is my family.
Le presento a mi familia.
I'd like you to meet my family.
Me gustaría que conociera a mi familia.

☞ *Now introduce these members of your family.*

your sister	<u>Le presento a mi hermana.</u>
your father	<u>Le presento a mi padre.</u>
your aunt	<u>Le presento a mi tía.</u>
your cousins	<u>Le presento a mis primos.</u>

♪ My family!
¡Mi familia!
This is my family.
Le presento a mi familia.
I'd like you to meet my family.
Me gustaría que conociera a mi familia.

Repeat these questions in Spanish.

What's your name?	¿Cómo se llama usted?
What's his name?	¿Cómo se llama él?
What's her name?	¿Cómo se llama ella?

Now repeat these answers in Spanish.

My name is Jon.	Me llamo Jon.
His name is Jon.	Se llama Jon.
My name is Melissa.	Me llamo Melissa.
Her name is Melissa.	Se llama Melissa.

♪ My family!
¡Mi familia!
This is my family.
Le presento a mi familia.
I'd like you to meet my family.
Me gustaría que conociera a mi familia.

How old are you?	¿Cuántos años tiene usted?
How old is he?	¿Cuántos años tiene él?
How old is she?	¿Cuántos años tiene ella?
I'm seventeen.	Tengo diecisiete años.
I'm seventy.	Tengo setenta años.
He's fourteen.	Él tiene catorce años.
She's forty.	Ella tiene cuarenta años.

Repeat these numbers in Spanish.

eleven	once
twelve	doce
thirteen	trece
fourteen	catorce
fifteen	quince
sixteen	dieciséis
seventeen	diecisiete
eighteen	dieciocho
nineteen	diecinueve
twenty	veinte
thirty	treinta
forty	cuarenta
fifty	cincuenta
sixty	sesenta
seventy	setenta
eighty	ochenta
ninety	noventa
a hundred	cien

Now repeat these questions in Spanish.

How old are you?	¿Cuántos años tiene usted?
How old is he?	¿Cuántos años tiene él?
How old is she?	¿Cuántos años tiene ella?

And now repeat these answers.

I'm twenty years old.	Tengo veinte años.
I'm thirty years old.	Tengo treinta años.
I'm forty.	Tengo cuarenta años.
He's fifty years old.	Él tiene cincuenta años.
She's sixty years old.	Ella tiene sesenta años.
He's seventy.	Él tiene setenta años.
She's eighty.	Ella tiene ochenta años.

My family!
¡Mi familia!
This is my family.
Le presento a mi familia.
I'd like you to meet my family.
Me gustaría que conociera a mi familia.
Me gustaría que conociera a mi familia.

¡Mucho gusto!
¡El gusto es mío!

AT THE DINNER TABLE.

Melissa:	Please pass the salt.
Jon:	Here you go.
Melissa:	Thanks.
Jon:	This is a beautiful meal, Mom.
Guests:	Wonderful. Delicious. Perfect.
Mom:	Well, this is a beautiful family.
Melissa:	But *some* of us are a little weird…Johnny.
Jon:	Are you talking to me?
Melissa:	You suddenly have this uncontrollable urge to study Spanish? What's *that* about?
Jon:	Well…you see…I met this girl.
Melissa:	I knew it! I knew it! I knew it!
Mom:	So what's she like, Jonathan?
Jon:	Like a dream.

♪ She's beautiful.
Ella es bella.
♪ She's smart.
Es inteligente.
♪ She's funny.
Es divertida.
♪ She's sincere.
Es sincera.
♪ She's kind.
Es amable.
♪ She's calm.
Es tranquila.
♪ And my heart knows when she's near.
Y mi corazón sabe cuando está cerca.

♪ Like a dream!
¡Como un sueño!

She is
Ella es
like a dream
como un sueño
to me.
para mí.
Like a dream,
Como un sueño,
she comes.
ella viene.
And suddenly,
Y de repente,
like a dream,
como un sueño,
she answers my prayer.
ella contesta a mis plegarias.

And I see her everywhere,
Y la veo por todas partes,
like a dream.
como un sueño.

Melissa:	So is this just another wild fantasy, brother dear, or is the feeling mutual?
Jon:	I don't know.
Sr. González:	No sé.
Jon:	I think so.
Sr. González:	Creo que sí.
Jon:	I hope so.
Sr. González:	Espero que sí.

He's handsome.
Él es guapo.
He's smart.
Es inteligente.
He's funny.
Es divertido.
He's sincere.
Es sincero.
He's kind.
Es amable.
He's calm.
Es tranquilo.
And my heart knows when he's near.
Y mi corazón sabe cuando está cerca.

Like a dream!
¡Como un sueño!
He is
Él es
like a dream
como un sueño
to me.
para mí.
Like a dream,
Como un sueño,
he comes.
él viene.
And suddenly,
Y de repente,
like a dream,
como un sueño,
he answers my prayer.
él contesta a mis plegarias.

> And I see him everywhere,
> Y lo veo por todas partes,
> like a dream.
> como un sueño.

Melissa:	So what's your dreamgirl's name?
Jon:	Elena.
Melissa:	And what does she look like? Is she tall?
Jon:	She's tall. But not too tall.
Melissa:	Is she thin?
Jon:	She's thin. But not too thin.

Describe the people you know. Listen, and repeat the Spanish.

He's tall.	Él es alto.
She's tall.	Ella es alta.
He's short.	Él es bajo.
She's short.	Ella es baja.
He's thin.	Él es delgado.
She's thin.	Ella es delgada.
He's fat.	Él es gordo.
She's fat.	Ella es gorda.
He's strong.	Él es fuerte.
She's strong.	Ella es fuerte.
He's sick.	Él está enfermo.
She's sick.	Ella está enferma.
He's old.	Él es mayor.
She's old.	Ella es mayor.
He's young.	Él es joven.
She's young.	Ella es joven.
He's rich.	Él es rico.

She's rich.	Ella es rica.
He's poor.	Él es pobre.
She's poor.	Ella es pobre.

Melissa: Johnny, do we all get to meet Elena anytime soon?

Jon: I'm going to see her this weekend. Talk to me on Monday.

Dad: Everything happens when the time is right.

Mom: And if it's right, you'll know.

Dad: Just like your mom and I knew...all those centuries ago.

Like a dream!
¡Como un sueño!
He is...
Él es...
She is...
Ella es...
like a dream...
como un sueño...
to me...
para mí...
to me.
para mí.
Like a dream,
Como un sueño,
he comes...
él viene...
she comes.
ella viene.
And suddenly,
Y de repente,
like a dream,

como un sueño,
he answers my prayer...
él contesta a mis plegarias...
she answers my prayer.
ella contesta a mis plegarias.
And I see him everywhere...
Y lo veo por todas partes...
And I see her everywhere,
Y la veo por todas partes,
like a dream.
como un sueño.
Like a dream!
¡Como un sueño!
Like a dream!
¡Como un sueño!
Like a dream!
¡Como un sueño!

Show ⟨10⟩

Just for Fun

LATER THAT NIGHT, JON RETURNS HOME.

Jon:	Home at last.
Sr. González:	¡Bienvenido! ¡Bienvenido a tu casa!
Jon:	Señor González! Are you still hanging around?
Sr. González:	Are you saying you're tired of my company?
Jon:	No, I'm just tired.
Sr. González:	Estoy cansado.
Jon:	Yes! ¡Estoy cansado! ¡Estoy muy cansado!
Sr. González:	So good night! ¡Buenas noches!
Jon:	No, wait!
Sr. González:	¡Espera! But to me, *you* should say, "Espere." Show some respect.
Jon:	Espere…por favor. Just one more favor.
Sr. González:	¿Sí?
Jon:	A little advice.
Sr. González:	Just call her.
Jon:	¿Perdón? What are you, a mind reader?
Sr. González:	No, I'm a Spanish teacher, remember?
Jon:	Well…I was *supposed* to call Elena at her office *tomorrow*.
Sr. González:	When?
Jon:	Tomorrow.
Sr. González:	¡Mañana!
Jon:	Mañana. Mañana.
Sr. González:	It's OK.
Jon:	What?

Sr. González:	You can call her now.
Jon:	¿Ahora?
Sr. González:	¡Ahora!

I'm happy! I'm sad!
I'm nervous. I'm mad.
I'm excited!
I'm delighted!
That's good! That's bad!
I'm tired! I'm wide awake!
And everything feels right!
I'm in love!
¡Estoy enamorado!
I love you!
¡Te quiero!
I'm in love…
¡Estoy enamorado
esta noche!
tonight!

*So how do you feel? Repeat the sentences in Spanish—
after the man or after the woman.*

I'm happy.	Estoy feliz.
	Estoy feliz.
I'm sad.	Estoy triste.
	Estoy triste.
I'm nervous.	Estoy nervioso.
	Estoy nerviosa.
I'm mad.	Estoy enojado.
	Estoy enojada.
I'm excited.	Estoy entusiasmado.
	Estoy entusiasmada.

I'm delighted.	Estoy encantado.
	Estoy encantada.
I'm in love.	Estoy enamorado.
	Estoy enamorada.

I'm in love…
Estoy enamorado…
I'm in love…
Estoy enamorada…
We're in love…
¡Estamos enamorados
esta noche!
tonight!

JON MAKES A PHONE CALL.

Elena:	¿Aló?
Jon:	Elena?
Elena:	Ah, Jon. How are you? ¿Cómo estás?
Jon:	Fine. Fine. Bien, bien.
Elena:	What's new? ¿Qué hay de nuevo?
Jon:	Nothing much.
Sr. González:	Nada.
Elena:	How's your family? ¿Cómo está tu familia?
Jon:	Everyone's fine, thanks.
Sr. González:	Todos bien, gracias.
Jon:	They want to meet you.
Sr. González:	Ellos quisieran conocerte.
Elena:	Really? ¿De verdad?
Jon:	Well, maybe one day.
Sr. González:	Algún día.

Jon:	Anyway, I'm sorry.
Sr. González:	Lo siento.
Elena:	¿Lo sientes? ¿Por qué? Why?
Jon:	For calling now.
Sr. González:	Por llamarte a esta hora.
Jon:	It's late.
Sr. González:	Es tarde.
Elena:	No…es *temprano*. It's early. For me. Para mí. Me alegra que me hayas llamado. I'm glad you called.
Jon:	Really?
Sr. González:	¿De verdad?
Elena:	Really. De verdad. So…entonces…what do you want to do this weekend? ¿Qué quieres hacer este fin de semana?
Jon:	Whatever you like.
Sr. González:	Lo que tú quieras.
Elena:	Well…bueno…there are lots of possibilities! ¡Hay muchas posibilidades!

What do you want to do?
¿Qué quieres hacer?
Whatever you like!
¡Lo que tú quieras!
What do you want to do together?
¿Qué quieres hacer juntos?

I don't care!
¡Cualquier cosa!
It's up to you!
¡Lo que tú digas!

Let's go to the movies!
Let's go to the zoo!

🎵 ¡Vamos al cine!
🎵 ¡Vamos al zoológico!
🎵 We could go to a museum
🎵 and the theater, too.
🎵 Podríamos ir a un museo
🎵 y al teatro también.
🎵 Or maybe to the park?
🎵 ¿O quizás al parque?
🎵 What do you want to do?
🎵 And after dark,
🎵 Y cuando oscurezca....
🎵 what do you want to do?

What do you want to do? Repeat these suggestions in Spanish.

Why don't we go to the movies?	¿Por qué no vamos al cine?
Why don't we go to the zoo?	¿Por qué no vamos al zoológico?
Why don't we go to a museum?	¿Por qué no vamos a un museo?
Why don't we go to the theater?	¿Por qué no vamos al teatro?
Why don't we go to the park?	¿Por qué no vamos al parque?

Jon: Or we could just spend a quiet day...or evening...at home.

Elena: Well...we could.

Repeat these activities in Spanish.

read a book	**leer un libro**
We could read a book.	**Podríamos leer un libro.**
watch TV	**ver televisión**
We could watch TV.	**Podríamos ver televisión.**
listen to music	**escuchar música**
We could listen to music.	**Podríamos escuchar música.**
play cards	**jugar cartas**
We could play cards.	**Podríamos jugar cartas.**
play with the computer	**jugar con la computadora**
We could play with the computer.	**Podríamos jugar con la computadora.**
study Spanish	**estudiar español**
We could study Spanish.	**Podríamos estudiar español.**

Elena: How about something more physical! What sports do you like?

Repeat the Spanish.

basketball	**baloncesto**
Do you like basketball?	**¿Te gusta el baloncesto?**
I like basketball.	**Me gusta el baloncesto.**
soccer	**fútbol**
Do you like soccer?	**¿Te gusta el fútbol?**
I like soccer.	**Me gusta el fútbol.**
tennis	**tenis**
Do you like tennis?	**¿Te gusta el tenis?**
I like tennis.	**Me gusta el tenis.**
football	**fútbol americano**
Do you like football?	**¿Te gusta el fútbol americano?**

I don't like football.	No me gusta el fútbol americano.
golf	golf
Do you like golf?	¿Te gusta el golf?
I don't like golf.	No me gusta el golf.
baseball	béisbol
Do you like baseball?	¿Te gusta el béisbol?
I don't like baseball.	No me gusta el béisbol.

Jon: Something tells me we have a lot in common!

What do you want to do?
¿Qué quieres hacer?
Whatever you like!
¡Lo que tú quieras!
What do you want to do together?
¿Qué quieres hacer juntos?

I don't care!
¡Cualquier cosa!
It's up to you!
¡Lo que tú digas!
Let's go to the movies!
Let's go to the zoo!
¡Vamos al cine!
¡Vamos al zoológico!
We could go to a museum
and the theater, too.
Podríamos ir a un museo
y al teatro también.
Or maybe to the park?
¿O quizás al parque?
What do you want to do?

♪ And after dark,
Y cuando oscurezca...
𝄢 what do you want to do?

Elena:	Tengo una buena idea. I have a good idea. It's good...es bueno...for your body...para el cuerpo...*and* for your soul...y para el espíritu. Do you like to...dance? ¿Te gusta bailar?
Jon:	I *love* to dance!
Sr. González:	¡Me encanta bailar!
Jon:	¡Me encanta bailar!

♪ Dance with me!
Dance with me!
♪ Feel the beat!
♪ Dance with me!

♪ ¡Baila conmigo!
♪ ¡Baila conmigo!
♪ ¡Siente el ritmo!
♪ ¡Baila conmigo!

♪ Move with me!
♪ Move with me!
Feel the beat!
♪ Dance with me!

♪ ¡Muévete conmigo!
♪ ¡Muévete conmigo!
♪ ¡Siente el ritmo!
𝄢 ¡Baila conmigo!

Hold me now!
Hold me now!
Feel the beat!
Dance with me!

¡Abrázame ahora!
¡Abrázame ahora!
¡Siente el ritmo!
¡Baila conmigo!

Kiss me now!
Kiss me now!
Feel the beat!
Dance with me!

¡Bésame ahora!
¡Bésame ahora!
¡Siente el ritmo!
¡Baila conmigo!

Touch me now!
Touch me now!
Feel the heat!
Dance with me!

¡Tócame ahora!
¡Tócame ahora!
¡Siente el calor!
¡Baila conmigo!

Move your body! Repeat the words in Spanish.

my arms	mis brazos
my legs	mis piernas
my hands	mis manos
my feet	mis pies
my head	mi cabeza
my eyes	mis ojos
my mouth	mi boca
my nose	mi nariz
my ears	mis orejas
my back	mi espalda
my chest	mi pecho
my shoulders	mis hombros
Dance with me!	¡Baila conmigo!
Move with me!	¡Muévete conmigo!
Hold me now!	¡Abrázame ahora!
Kiss me now!	¡Bésame ahora!
Touch me now!	¡Tócame ahora!
Feel the beat!	¡Siente el ritmo!
Feel the heat!	¡Siente el calor!

Dance with me!
Dance with me!
Feel the beat!
Dance with me!

¡Baila conmigo!
¡Baila conmigo!
¡Siente el ritmo!
¡Baila conmigo!

Jon:	Saturday night?
Elena:	¿El sábado por la noche? Great! ¡Fabuloso!
Jon:	And Señor González…muchas gracias. You're a wonderful teacher!
Sr. González:	Un profesor maravilloso. Yo lo sé. I know.
Jon:	And I'm really grateful for all your help.
Sr. González:	Le agradezco mucho toda su ayuda.
Jon:	Le agradezco mucho toda su ayuda.
Sr. González:	Oh, don't mention it. No hay de que.
Jon:	But you're not coming on my date with me!
Sr. González:	Oh, it's OK, Jon. My work with you is done…for now. And anyway…I'm leaving you in very capable hands! Right? ¿Verdad?

¡Baila conmigo!
¡Baila conmigo!
¡Siente el ritmo!
¡Baila conmigo!

¡Muévete conmigo!
¡Muévete conmigo!
¡Siente el ritmo!
¡Baila conmigo!

¡Abrázame ahora!
¡Abrázame ahora!
¡Siente el ritmo!
¡Baila conmigo!

¡Bésame ahora!
¡Bésame ahora!
¡Siente el ritmo!
¡Baila conmigo!

¡Tócame ahora!
¡Tócame ahora!
¡Siente el calor!
¡Baila conmigo!

¡Baila conmigo!
¡Baila conmigo!
¡Siente el ritmo!
Dance with me!

Mini-Grammar

Articles

Nouns in Spanish are either masculine or feminine. Articles agree in gender and number with the noun.

1. **Definite article** (the):

	singular		plural	
masc.	*el* **tren**	the train	*los* **trenes**	the trains
fem.	*la* **casa**	the house	*las* **casas**	the houses

2. **Indefinite article** (a/an):

masc.	*un* **lápiz**	a pencil	*unos* **lápices**	some pencils
fem.	*una* **mesa**	a table	*unas* **mesas**	some tables

Nouns

1. Most nouns which end in **o** are masculine. Those ending in **a** are generally feminine.

2. Normally, nouns which end in a vowel add **s** to form the plural; nouns ending in a consonant add **es**.

3. To show possession, use the preposition **de** (of).

el fin *de* **la fiesta**	the end of the party
el principio *del** **mes**	the beginning of the month
las maletas *de* **los viajeros**	the travelers' suitcases
los ojos *de* **las niñas**	the girls' eyes
el cuarto *de* **Roberto**	Robert's room

* (**del** is the contraction of **de** + **el**)

Adjectives

1. Adjectives agree with the noun in gender and number. If the masculine form ends in **o**, the feminine ends in **a**. As a rule, the adjective comes after the noun.

el niño pequeño	the small boy
la niña pequeña	the small girl

2. If the masculine form of the adjective ends in **e** or with a consonant, the feminine form is generally the same.

el muro/la casa grande	the big wall/house
el mar/la flor azul	the blue sea/flower

3. Most adjectives form their plurals in the same way as nouns.

un carro rojo	a red car
dos carros rojos	two red cars

4. **Possessive adjectives** agree with the thing possessed.

	sing.	plur.
my	**mi**	**mis**
your (inform.)	**tu**	**tus**
your (form.)	**su**	**sus**
his/her/its	**su**	**sus**
our	**nuestro(a)**	**nuestros(as)**
your (pl.)	**su**	**sus**
their	**su**	**sus**

su hijo	his or her or their son
sus brazos	his or her or their arms*

   *Spanish often uses the definite article where a possessive adjective would be used in English.

Me duele la cabeza.	My head hurts.

5. **Comparative** and **superlative** are formed by adding **más** (more) or **menos** (less), **lo más** or **lo menos** before the adjective.

   alto high   **más** alto higher   **lo más** alto highest

Adverbs

These are formed by adding -**mente** to the feminine form of the adjective (if it differs from the masculine); otherwise add -**mente** to the masculine form.

sincero(a) sincere **fácil** easy
sinceramente sincerely **fácilmente** easily

Possessive pronouns

	sing.	plur.
mine	**mío(a)**	**míos (as)**
yours (inf. sing.)	**tuyo(a)**	**tuyos(as)**
yours (form.)	**suyo(a)**	**suyos(as)**
his/hers/its	**suyo(a)**	**suyos(as)**
ours	**nuestro(a)**	**nuestros(as)**
yours (pl.)	**suyo(a)**	**suyos(as)**
theirs	**suyo(a)**	**suyos(as)**

Demonstrative pronouns

	masc.	fem.	neut.
this	**éste**	**ésta**	**esto**
these	**éstos**	**éstas**	**estos**
that	**ése/aquél**	**ésa/aquélla**	**eso/aquello**
those	**ésos/aquéllos**	**ésas/aquéllas**	**esos/aquellos**

The masc. and fem. forms are also used as demonstrative adjectives, without accents.

Esos libros no me gustan. I don't like those books.
Eso no me gusta. I don't like that.

Personal pronouns

	subject	direct object	indirect object
I	**yo**	**me**	**me**
you	**tú**	**te**	**te**

you	usted	lo	le
he	él	lo	le
she	ella	la	le
it*		lo/la	le
we	nosotros(as)	nos	nos
you (pl.)	ustedes	los	les
they	ellos(as)	los	les

Subject pronouns are generally omitted, except in the polite you-form (**usted, ustedes**). **Tú** is used when talking to a relative, close friends, and children and between young people; **usted** and the plural **ustedes** are used in all other cases.

*Spanish does not use a subject pronoun for the meaning of *it.*. The subject is omitted.

El libro es interesante.	The book is interesting.
Es interesante.	It's interesting.

Negatives

Negatives are formed by placing **no** before the verb.

Es nuevo. It's new. **No es nuevo.** It's not new.

Questions

In Spanish, questions are often formed by changing the intonation of your voice. Very often, the personal pronoun is left out, both in affirmative sentences and in questions.

Hablo español.	I speak Spanish.
¿Habla español?	Do you speak Spanish?

Note the double question mark used in Spanish. The same is true of exclamation marks.

¡Qué sofá tan lindo!	What a nice couch!

Drive & Learn
Phrases

Here are useful Spanish expressions from the ten *Drive & Learn Spanish* shows. The English equivalents are not word-for-word translations, but they are functional equivalents. In other words, you may use each Spanish phrase in the same situation as you would use the English expression beside it.

SHOW 1   Getting Started

Mucho gusto. It's nice to meet you.

El gusto es mío. It's nice to meet you, too.

Me llamo (Jon). My name is (Jon).

¿De dónde es usted? Where do come you from?

Soy de (Nueva York). I'm from (New York).

¿Qué hora es? What time is it?

Es la una. It's one o'clock.

Son las (dos/tres/cuatro). It's (two/three/four) o'clock.

Muchas gracias. Thank you very much.

De nada. You're welcome.

¿Dónde está? Where is it?

¿Dónde está (el jabón)? Where's (the soap)?

Está aquí. It's here.

Está allí. It's there.

SHOW 2 Ready to Leave

¿Tiene hambre/sed? Are you hungry/thirsty?

Tengo hambre/sed. I'm hungry/thirsty.

Buen provecho. Enjoy your meal.

¿Qué tiempo hace? How's the weather?

¿Qué pasa? What's happening?

Hace buen tiempo. The weather is nice.

Hace mal tiempo. The weather is bad.

Hace calor/frío/sol/viento. It's warm/cold/sunny/windy.

Está nublado/lloviendo/nevando. It's cloudy/raining/snowing.

¿Cómo se llega allá? How do I get there?

en tren/autobús/carro by train/bus/car

por avión by plane

a pie on foot

SHOW 3 On the Street

Quisiera (un boleto), por favor. I'd like (one ticket), please.

Se hace tarde. It's getting late.

¡Vámonos! Let's go!

¡Apurémosnos! Hurry up!

de ida one way

de ida y vuelta round trip

¿Cuánto cuesta? How much is that?

¿A qué hora (sale el próximo tren)? What time (is the next train)?

a las (siete) y diez/cuarto/veinte/media at (seven) ten/fifteen/twenty/thirty

a las (ocho) menos veinte/cuarto at twenty to/a quarter to (eight)

¿Cómo está? How are you? *(formal)*

¿Cómo estás? How are you? *(informal)*

Muy bien. I'm fine.

Bastante bien. Pretty good.

Quisiera presentarle a (mi amigo). I'd like you to meet (my friend).

Éste es (Jon). This is (Jon).

Un placer conocerle. A pleasure meeting you.

Igualmente. Same here.

Nos vemos. See you soon.

¿Le gustaría…? Do you want…?

Me encantaría. I'd love to.

¿Qué le parece…? How about…?

Hasta luego. See you later.

SHOW 4   At Work

tiempo libre free time

No tengo (tiempo). I don't have (time).

¿Qué hace usted? What do you do? *(formal)*

¿Qué haces tú? What do you do? *(informal)*

Soy (médico). I am (a doctor).

¡Cómo no!/¡Por supuesto! Of course!

¡Claro! Sure!

¿Me presta (su bolígrafo) por favor? Can I borrow your (pen), please?

SHOW 5 Lunch Hour

Una mesa para dos. A table for two.

¿Y usted? And you? *(formal)*

¿Y tú? And you? *(informal)*

¿Qué quieres? What would you like? *(informal)*

¿Quisiera ordenar? Are you ready to order?

¿Qué desearía tomar? What would you like to drink?

¿Qué le gustaría ordenar? What would you like to order?

Quisiera (una ensalada). I'll have (a salad).

Me gustaría (una ensalada). I'd like (a salad).

La cuenta, por favor. The check, please.

SHOW 6 On the Phone

A la orden. May I help you?

¿Puedo hablar con...? Can I speak to...?

¿Quién llama, por favor? Who's calling, please?

Un momento, por favor. Hold on, please.

El está ocupado en este momento. He can't come to the phone right now.

¿Desearía dejarle un mensaje? Would you like to leave a message?

Por favor, dígale que me llame. Please ask him/her to call me.

¿Cuál es su número de teléfono? What's your phone number?

Yo le daré su mensaje. I'll give him/her the message.

¡Eso es! That's it!

¡Hasta mañana! Till tomorrow!

SHOW 7   Around the Neighborhood

Es verdad. That's true.

derecho straight ahead

a la izquierda on the left

a la derecha on the right

en la esquina on the corner

a la vuelta de la esquina around the corner

enfrente across the street

Estoy buscando (el correo). I'm looking for (the post office).

Está muy cerca. It's very close.

¿Dónde está (la escuela) más cercana? Where's the nearest (school)?

Necesito comprar (estampillas). I need to buy (stamps).

Vamos (al correo). Let's go (to the post office).

¡Eso es todo! That's all!

SHOW 8   At Home

Dime, ¿porqué? Tell me why.

Bienvenido (a casa). Welcome (home).

¡Qué alegría (que estés aquí)! I'm so glad (you're here).

¡Siéntate! Have a seat! *(sentarse = to sit)*

¡Siéntete en tu casa! Make yourself at home. *(sentirse = to feel)*

Me encanta que te guste. So glad you like it.

Muy amable. That's very nice of you.

Me alegra que te sientas así. I'm glad you feel that way.

SHOW 9 Family Time

Le presento (a mi familia). This is (my family).

Me gustaría que conociera (a mi familia). I'd like you to meet (my family).

¿Cómo se llama usted? What's your name?

¿Cuántos años tiene usted? How old are you?

Tengo (diecisiete años). I'm (seventeen years old).

No sé. I don't know.

SHOW 10 Just for Fun

¿Qué hay de nuevo? What's new?

Nada. Nothing much.

Algún día. One day.

Lo que tú quieras. Whatever you like.

¿Qué quieres hacer juntos? What do you want to do together?

Cualquier cosa. I don't care.

Lo que tú digas. It's up to you.

Podríamos ir (a un museo). We could go (to a museum).

Por qué no vamos (al cine)? Why don't we go (to the movies)?

¿Verdad? Right?

Drive & Learn
Vocabulary

A

a, an **un(a)** *m,f* 12
accountant **contador(a)** *m,f* 32
across **enfrente** 57
actor **actor** *m* 33
actress **actriz** *f* 33
all **todo** 60
also, too **también** 53
always **siempre** 28
and **y** 13
answer **contestar** 78
appetizer **entrada** *f* 40
appointment **cita** *f* 29
April **abril** 30
armchair **sillón** *m* 65
arms **brazos** *m* 92
arrive **llegar** 18
attic **ático** *m* 65
August **agosto** 30
aunt **tía** *f* 73

B

back **espalda** *f* 92
backyard **patio** *m* 65
bad **mal** 16
bakery **panadería** *f* 59
bank **banco** *m* 55

baseball **béisbol** *m* 89
basement **sótano** *m* 65
basketball **baloncesto** *m* 88
bathroom **baño** *m* 64
be **ser** 4
be **estar** 5
beat, rhythm **ritmo** *m* 90
beautiful **bello(a)** 77
bed **cama** *f* 69
bedroom **cuarto** *m* 64
beer **cerveza** *f* 42
beige **beige** 12
bicycle **bicicleta** *f* 18
black **negro** 11
blanket **cobija** *f* 69
blue **azul** 11
boat **bote** *m* 18
body **cuerpo** *m* 90
book **libro** *m* 34
bookcase **estante de libros** *m* 65
bookstore **librería** *f* 57
borrow **prestar** 34
bottle **botella** f 42
boxes **cajas** *f* 69
boy **niño** *m* 71
bread **pan** *m* 60
breakfast **desayuno** *m* 26

dinner **cena** *f* 26
dishwasher **lavaplatos** *m* 67
do, make **hacer** 32
doctor **médico** *m,f* 32
drawer **gaveta** *f* 34
dream **sueño** *m* 77
dress **vestido** *m* 12
dresser **cómoda** *f* 69
drink **bebida** *f* 40
drink, take **tomar** 43

E

early **temprano** 86
ears **orejas** *m* 92
egg **huevo** *m* 14
eight **ocho** 1
eighteen **dieciocho** 75
eighty **ochenta** 75
eleven **once** 5
engineer **ingeniero(a)** *m,f* 33
excited **entusiasmado(a)** 84
expensive **caro** 60
eyes **ojos** *m* 92

F

fall **otoño** *m* 31
family **familia** *m* 72
fat **gordo(a)** 80
father **padre** *m* 73
February **febrero** 30
feel **sentir** 66
fifteen **quince** 75
fifty **cincuenta** 75
file **documento** *m* 36
file cabinet **archivador** *m* 36
first **primer** 22

fish **pescado** *m* 40
five **cinco** 1
florist **floristería** *f* 55
flower **flor** *f* 60
folder **carpeta** *f* 36
foot **pie** *m* 18
football **fútbol americano** *m* 88
for **para** 28
for **por** 93
fork **tenedor** *m* 40
forty **cuarenta** 75
four **cuatro** 1
fourteen **catorce** 75
free **libre** 28
french fries **papas fritas** *f* 42
Friday **viernes** 30
fried **frito** 14
friend **amigo(a)** *m,f* 23
from **de** 4
fruit **fruta** *f* 40
funny **divertido(a)** 77

G

garage **garaje** *m* 65
gift **regalo** *m* 61
gift shop **tienda de regalos** *f* 57
girl **niña** *f* 71
give **dar** 47
glass **vaso** *m* 40
golf **golf** *m* 89
good, well **bien** 4
good-bye **adiós, chao** 24
granddaughter **nieta** *f* 73
grandfather **abuelo** *m* 73
grandmother **abuela** *f* 73

grandson **nieto** *m* 73
gray **gris** 12
great **fabuloso** 93
green **verde** 12

H

half **media** 22
hamburger **hamburguesa** *f* 42
hands **manos** *f* 92
handsome **guapo** 79
happen **pasar** 71
happy **feliz** 84
(be) happy **alegrarse** 64
hat **sombrero** *m* 12
have **tener** 14
he **él** *m* 46
head **cabeza** *f* 92
heart **corazón** *m* 77
heat **calor** *m* 15
hello **aló** 46
help **ayuda** *f* 93
here **aquí** 6
hi **hola** 1
hold **abrazar** 91
home **casa** *f* 64
hope **esperar** 78
hospital **hospital** *m* 58
how **cómo** 18
how much **cuánto** 21
hundred **cien** 75
husband **esposo** *m* 73

I

I **yo** 47
idea **idea** *f* 90
in **adentro** 36

in love **enamorado(a)** 84
intelligent **inteligente** 77

J

jam **mermelada** *f* 13
January **enero** 30
juice **jugo** *m* 14
July **julio** 30
June **junio** 30

K

kind **amable** 77
kind, nice **amable** 66
kiss **besar** 91
kitchen **cocina** *f* 64
knife **cuchillo** *m* 40
know **saber** 77
know (a person) **conocer** 23

L

lamp **lámpara** *f* 65
last **último** 22
late **tarde** 20
lawyer **abogado(a)** *m,f* 32
leave **salir** 21
leave **dejar** 46
left **izquierda** 56
legs **piernas** *f* 92
library **biblioteca** *f* 56
life **vida** *f* 11
like **gustar** 24
listen **escuchar** 88
living room **sala** *f* 64
look for **buscar** 56
look, see **mirar** 11
love (to do something)

tired **cansado(a)** 83
toast **pan tostado** m 13
today **hoy** 16
together **juntos** 86
tomorrow **mañana** 54
toothbrush **cepillo de dientes** m 7
toothpaste **pasta de dientes** f 6
touch **tocar** 91
towel **toalla** f 7
train **tren** m 18
true **verdad** 55
Tuesday **martes** 29
turn **doblar** 57
twelve **doce** 5
twenty **veinte** 22
two **dos** 1

U

uncle **tío** m 73
under **debajo** 36
until **hasta** 23

V

vanilla ice cream **helado de vainilla** m 42
VCR **video** f 65
vegetable **vegetale** f 40
vegetable soup **sopa de verduras** f 42
very **muy** 3

W

waiter **camarero** m 43
want **querer** 20
weather **tiempo** m 16

Wednesday **miércoles** 29
week **semana** f 29
weekend **fin de semana** m 86
welcome **bienvenido** 64
what **qué** 5
whatever **cualquier** 86
when **cuando** 77
where **dónde** 4
which **cuál** 47
white **blanco** 11
who **quién** 46
why **por qué** 63
wife **esposa** f 73
window **ventana** f 65
windy **viento** 16
wine **vino** m 42
winter **invierno** m 31
wish, desire **desear** 43
with **con** 46
woman **mujer** f 71

Y

year **año** m 29
yellow **amarillo** 11
you **usted** (formal) 4
you **tú** (informal) 32
young **joven** 80
your **su** (formal) 34
your **tu** (informal) 64

Z

zoo **zoológico** m 87